⊖ AN OBSERVER'S

Drawing wit

CW00793972

⊕ OBSERVER'S GUIDES

Home and Garden

The Herb Grower's Guide
Car Care

Art and Craft

Pencil Drawing
Drawing with Ink
Using Pastels
Beginning Watercolour
Materials and Techniques of Oil Painting
Materials and Techniques of Watercolour
Materials and Techniques of Acrylic Painting
Materials and Techniques of Collage
Let's Make Pottery

Where Is It?

British Paintings—Hogarth to Turner
European Paintings of the Eighteenth Century
Twentieth Century Paintings—Bonnard to Rothko
Italian, French and Spanish Paintings of the 17th Century

DRAWING WITH INK

J. C. Brobbel, A.R.B.A.

FREDERICK WARNE

Published by Frederick Warne (Publishers) Ltd, London, 1981

To my parents, for their support and patience

Acknowledgements

The British Museum: Rembrandt, Michelangelo, Claude, Kollwitz, Chadel; Ashmolean Museum: Samuel Palmer; Courtauld Institute: Van Gogh; Witt Library: Van Gogh drawing and fig. 42; *Artist* magazine for figs. 25 and 28; Pauline Sandor; Margaret Ford for *Study for Mural*

ISBN 0 7232 2468 4

Printed in Great Britain by
BAS Printers Limited, Over Wallop, Hampshire
1502.1180

Contents

Introduction

Since the introduction of the graphite pencil the use of ink as a drawing medium has declined considerably; more so in the fine arts however, as it is still used to great effect and advantage in graphic art. For the novice, ink drawing, especially pen and ink, appears to be a daunting prospect, and as a consequence the student portfolio often lacks examples of such work.

Its very positive and permanent nature makes pen and ink difficult to erase and alter in the way mistakes in pencil drawing can be corrected and redrawn. Working with pen, ink and wash needs careful forethought and decisiveness in execution from the very outset. The student must not be too bothered if first attempts prove to be awkward and a little rigid. This is only natural, and it is important to give oneself sufficient time to get to know the medium, and what it is capable of once the technicalities are understood. Even though a student may be adept at using pencil, the problems of a new medium must be tackled with a certain humility, in that it will teach entirely new approaches to familiar subjects. It takes more time than one ever imagines to really learn about new media, and so patience is essential if one is to discover what pen, ink and wash can do to improve one's draughtsmanship.

Most of the instruction in this short book will be in the use of metal-nib pens and brush, though quills and reed pens will be discussed. This is mainly because quills and reeds are more difficult to find. However, those students wishing to manufacture their own will be instructed.

Although this book only deals with monochrome ink drawing it does not follow that this is the only arrangement. Those students wishing to experiment with coloured inks will find many of the techniques employed in monochrome drawing both suitable and adaptable to coloured ink work.

Pen, ink and wash was, with crayon, the most widely used medium until the 19th century. Amongst the greatest exponents of its techniques were Michelangelo, Rembrandt, and Claude Lorraine, whose drawings are certainly worth study if one's examination of this medium is to be comprehensive. Kathë Kollwitz the 20th-century German etcher was a superb draughtsman and many of her preliminary drawings were made in pen, ink and wash.

Rembrandt. *Two negro drummers on mules.* Pen and wash, red chalk, yellow watercolour and touches of white

(British Museum)

Materials and using them

Nibs

Metal   Amongst the most useful of nibs is the ordinary school dipping nib. These are easily acquired and quite often spare nibs of varying thickness are supplied with the shaft. It is usually better to buy a shaft with a reservoir attached to it as these tend to be easier to clean than those which attach directly to the nibs. A small mapping pen is extremely useful and not too scratchy, if used gently. Both of these nibs are the dipping type.

Other metal-nibbed pens such as fountain pens or cartridge drawing pens can be useful, but the trouble with a fountain pen is that the ink has to be fairly thin in order to flow from its reservoir in the barrel to the nib. This means very black Indian ink cannot be used unless it is specially treated, and of course, this proves expensive. Cartridge drawing pens are very high standard instruments used in technical drawing. They work on the fountain pen principle and give a very even line which cannot be varied by adding pressure in the manner of the conventional dip pen. Though ideal for technical work, for freehand drawing the use of this type of nib is limited, especially as the nib must be held almost at right-angles to the drawing surface in order for the ink to flow evenly.

Reed   A reed pen is particularly good for ink drawing; the range of marks and its sensitivity make the instrument a pleasure to manipulate. However, it has the disadvantage of wearing out quickly. A reed pen can be made by picking suitable reeds growing by the river, or selecting thin bamboo, and sharpening the end into the shape of nib required. Split the nib about 6 mm ($\frac{1}{4}$ in) back from the point, and use it in the same way as a metal-nibbed pen. Reed gives a softer-edged line than metal and the thickness of strokes can be most variable.

Quills   A quill pen is made in the same way, from pinion feathers, and again it is a very pleasant experience to use one. It is possible to attach a metal reservoir to these types of pen, but it is not necessary. Make some yourself and see how you like the feel.

Biros and felt-tips   Biro pens and felt-tipped pens can be most effective

9

when used correctly – though they are limited slightly by their inflexibility and at times uneven flow.

Experiment with as many different pens and nibs as you can lay your hands on. Sometimes a number of different nibs may be used in the rendering of one drawing, and to good effect. Always rinse and dry nibs after use.

Inks

There are many colours of ink. The best and most graphic is Indian ink, which is black. When buying inks make sure that you are buying as good a quality as can be manufactured as many of the coloured inks fade quite quickly.

Brushes

Brushes for working with washes should be good quality red sable which can be shaped into a good point for fine work. Squirrel hair brushes can be used for larger areas and dry brush techniques. You will require sizes from three to eight for the sables, and larger for the squirrel hairs. Sable brushes are expensive but worth every penny, as they will last a lifetime if used and looked after carefully; they are indispensable for good quality work. Thoroughly wash out any sediment from the brushes after use.

Study in ball-point pen

Nude, felt-tip

Paper

The paper you use for pen and ink is really a personal choice. The most commonly used are hot pressed smooth papers, or the Bristol board used for illustration. It will be worthwhile trying different types of surface. Papers with heavy grain, though useful, can cause the pen to leave an interrupted line, and a metal pen can pick off parts of the raised surface if not used sensitively. Of course there are advantages with this type of paper which can be exploited.

Ingres papers can be a good surface to work on as the quality is good and the texture not too rough. Confine your first drawings in ink to white or off-white papers as coloured papers tend to give a false impression of the drawing's real quality.

Wash drawing needs a heavier paper and a good quality hand-made paper is best.

Other items

A good drawing board is essential, as is an assortment of linen rags and others with interesting textures. Sponges of various sizes are needed for mopping up and taking off areas of wash which are too dark, and a razor blade is useful for scraping away any areas which you have inadvertently made a tone which should be white. Gum strip 5 cm (2 in) wide is used in stretching papers for wash work. A large plate or similar will be needed to mix washes on, and an HB pencil for mapping out any construction lines you may want to use.

The pen as a drawing instrument is ideal. It is is the perfect instrument for crisp and clear statements. What seems to be its main disadvantage to most students is in fact its advantage – its marks cannot be eliminated. The struggle for accuracy is more apparent in pen and ink than in most other media. It is a myth that the great draughtsmen could draw whatever they wanted to, correctly and easily. If you look at any study in ink by a great master it shows much re-drawing and searching for the true line and tone. Once you realise that most good drawing is due to hard work, concentration and a will to 'get it right' you will have made a major breakthrough in your studies. Michelangelo is supposed to have said that his work contained 99 per cent hard work and one per cent genius. The significance of a remark like this by an artist as universal as Michelangelo is important to the student, not only because there is much truth in it, but also because it is a great inspiration to all of us to hear a man of such talent express such humility.

It does not matter if you draw the wrong shapes or lines in the wrong place, as long as you change them to their correct places. The viewer will automatically select the right ones. If you wish to make a drawing as a finished piece of work then the studies can be copied omitting the parts that are wrong. Your mistakes will be your greatest teaching, so try to use them to learn from.

An instrument as positive as the pen must be used in an equally positive way. This approach will perhaps take time to develop, but eventually it will become apparent that the best results are achieved by attacking your work with clear intentions concerning the approach which is to be used. Before ever putting pen to paper try to visualise how you wish to treat the subject. Do you think it requires a lot of tone, if so should you use single lines running parallel to each other, a dotted tonal structure, perhaps cross-hatching, or solid areas? As well as this type of consideration you will have to think about how you want to treat any contours or other areas which suggest a linear approach. Will you treat them as flowing lines, broken lines, a mixture of the two or some other way? If you do not keep on checking as the drawing progresses, and considering the unity, then there is a danger that you may end up with too many different approaches in one drawing. There is nothing wrong with being slow and deliberate; in fact it will be a great asset to you, so never rush a drawing; consider every mark you intend to make. Speed may come with experience, but it is not something for the student of drawing to 'learn'.

The pen is held in the same way as if writing, that is between the forefinger and thumb. In order that you do not damage the nib always pull the pen so that the nib follows the shaft and never leads. It should be held so the tip is always at right angles to the direction of the lines you are drawing. As with pencil one moves not just the hand but the whole arm, except when working on small areas.

There are a great many variations to how you manipulate the pen. Practise different strokes on any spare sheets of paper, varying the pressure you put on the nib. Make copies of these strokes and experiment with creating the textures in the illustration.

Occasionally the form of an object, as it turns away from the spectator, appears to lose its contour at certain points; the omission of the line at these points helps to suggest the turning away of the form in drawing. As well as these types of mark the dotted and dashed line can be very useful, especially for plotting the main directions of contours.

Creating the necessary tones in pen drawing is a lengthy process. Any errors you may make can often be concealed, for the black marks you first make on your paper are never as prominent again as the work progresses. A pen and ink drawing can be worked on for a very long time before it will break down. Furthermore it is possible to glue a clean piece of paper over

mapping pen

stipple

form indicated by line

reed

brush

13

those parts of a drawing which have broken down and continue with it in order to reach a conclusion, and it is certainly worth while doing this if you want to save a drawing and make it work.

Brushwork

One can use the brush both on its own and in conjunction with the pen. Together they form a very compatible relationship. Do not make the mistake of using too large a brush or too small a brush for the specific area you wish to wash over. When using the brush to draw lines the width of the brush should be used. The point can be useful for drawing thin lines but whenever possible the brush is best employed at its full width if you wish to get an even line, or paint up to an edge. For very fine lines it is probably best to revert to using the pen which can be more easily controlled because of its rigidity. A brush is employed for lines which vary their thickness to quite an extent and for large areas of tone.

Washes, which are in fact a series of glazes, can be built up gradually or laid in at the outset at the required depth – though this can only be achieved satisfactorily after much practice. To begin with I would suggest you build up your washes slowly. The illustration shows how you can do this and also how a dry brush can be used to achieve textures with wash. You may also want to experiment using different cloths as pads over the inked areas which can give a decorative effect to your drawing should you wish.

When laying in a wash keep it even and always wait until it is dry before laying subsequent washes. To achieve the best results the paper you use must be stretched on a drawing board in order that it dries flat without cockling. Paper which is not stretched can cause many problems when it becomes wet and pools of watery ink form in the cockles. These cockles will never dry out flat if the paper is not first stretched. Stretching your paper is comparatively easy. All you need is a drawing board or similar flat surface at least 5 cm (2 in) bigger all around than your paper size, a roll of 5 cm (2 in) brown gummed paper tape, and a sponge.

Soak the paper in a bath of water (or completely soak under a tap on both sides). When the paper is completely saturated lay it flat on your board. Having done this soak the tape and stick down the edges of the paper to the board. The tape should be half attached to the paper, and half to the board. The excess water which may be lying in pools on the surface can be gently sponged off – but do not rub the surface as it is at its most vulnerable state. Enthusiastic rubbing can destroy it. If you find the edges are cockled before sticking down do not try to smooth them out – stick on the tape over the cockles, but make sure it sticks to the paper everywhere it should. As the water evaporates the cockles will disappear from both paper and tape, resulting in a flat surface ideal for working on.

It is essential to carry out this operation swiftly, so have everything to hand with the tapes cut to size and ready to attach as soon as possible. Very large pieces of paper will need four hands as wet paper can tear and crease easily. You will get better at this procedure so do not be too alarmed if your first attempts are not too brilliant! Once the paper has been stretched it may be a couple of hours before the surface is dry enough again to work on. It is a good idea to stretch paper the previous day to ensure that it is ready. Drying the paper under great heat can be dangerous as it can cause splits to appear at the edges. Self-adhesive tape and masking tape are ineffective in stretching papers – the tape, like the paper, must shrink; and at the same rate.

All of this completed you will be ready to begin using washes. Small-size fairly heavy papers may not need to be stretched, and nor does Bristol board, though I do not find this surface particularly pleasant for working in washes with myself. However, try it and see how you get on as it can save time if you can only devote a few hours to drawing each week.

Flat washes are made by mixing up sufficient of the tone you want to begin with. Apply it to the paper as quickly and directly as possible. The main areas to watch out for are where pools form. You should eliminate these straight away by using a damp brush to lift them off. Remember wash always dries lighter, and you must take account of this when mixing. Dry brushwork can be most effective over flat washes.

Line

The most appropriate subjects to begin with, using the pen, are those most easily translated into linear terms. Bicycles are ideal and so are winter trees and fences. Choose subjects which are not too complicated. A branch of a tree, a sprig of holly, or some seashells can often make very beautiful drawings. If you can get hold of a corn on the cob this is a perfect subject to begin with.

Textures

Wash   The type of subject to choose when experimenting with textures should again be fairly simple and where possible single objects. Scissors and

A bicycle is a subject which lends itself to pen and ink drawing. The viewpoint of the artist is very close and there is obvious distortion to the back wheel because of this. It makes an interesting study, especially when the sizes of the wheels are compared. The difference between their sizes is much greater than expected when their close relationship is taken into account. It is possible to check the accuracy of such studies by looking at them upside down. Negative shape must be considered in such a drawing and in fact this is one which concerns itself almost exclusively with space between lines and not lines themselves.

This drawing would require almost no knowledge of perspective, had the viewpoint been moved slightly to the left. The drawing consists of lines, but concerns itself mainly with texture, built up gradually. Where lines are crossed to make texture the first strokes were left to dry before the overlapping ones were applied.

The figure, though 'travelling' into the picture, is still not satisfactory; because of his position under the tree an ambiguity has arisen: it appears to be growing out of his head. He would perhaps work better if a few steps further into the composition. The skyline would perhaps be better lower down; the picture is saved by the buildings on the right preventing the skyline from cutting the composition in two. Do you consider it a good or bad point that the four trees are almost exactly the same distance apart?

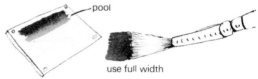

pool

use full width

Graded washes are achieved by first laying down a well loaded brush of pure black ink. When the stroke is finished raise the top of the board slightly so that the excess ink forms a pool along its bottom edge. Add a small quantity of water to the pure ink on your plate or palette and repeat the stroke allowing it to overlap the pool which has been formed. By adding a little clean water each time to the supply of ink on your plate and repeating this process you will soon be able to master graded washes. The important points to remember are: keep it wet; always try to make one stroke sufficient; keep the surface angled towards you and the pools fluent.

The final pool—which should be clear water—can be 'lifted' from the paper by gently passing a dried brush through it. If you find your washes are streaky it will be because either the wash is too dry, the water is dirty or the metal ferrule of the brush is scraping the paper.

Always leave washes flat so they dry evenly and do not run. When first completed your wash may look 'stringy' as if it is going to bleed into a flat tone. Do not try to alter it, leave it until it is dry—it will be all right.

metal teapots can make ideal subjects for rendering in wash. Other subjects which you could use to practise building up textures are brick walls – find a suitable demolition site and have a go at reproducing the textures which you find, especially where you have fireplaces and torn wallpaper. You could try using both pen and brush here.

Tone   To help you sort out tones in pen and wash you need only go as far as your bathroom. Make a drawing of the hand basin, taps and soap. Leave out anything which is multi-coloured such as face-cloths. This type of subject – which is all one colour – can be comparatively easy to translate into grey washes.

As a beginner you do not want to choose complicated subjects. In order that you can learn about the medium it is important that you minimise the draughting and that you are not too caught up with the problems of getting proportions right.

It can be observed that the changes in plane in this picture are shown by light areas more than by dark. The subject aside, it is a drawing of simple tonal values, sometimes graded and at other times quite positive. The divisions of the tiles help to establish the angles of the edges of the basin, and their darkness helps to 'throw' the form away from the wall. The shadows from the taps help to place them as upright forms.

19

Michelangelo: *Seated nude man turning away* (study for a figure in the foremost row of *The Bathers* cartoon). Pen and brush in two different coloured inks heightened with white.

(British Museum)

Preparation and selection

After you have worked from observation of real and tangible subjects for only a short time, it becomes apparent that a process of selection is necessary. What can be left out of a drawing? I have found that one of the best ways to tackle this problem is simply to draw everything that you possibly can, for only by putting down everything will you be able to learn what is essential. It will always be a problem; sometimes it can be resolved by re-drawing at a later stage in the studio.

A small drawing which attempts to portay something of the atmosphere on a particular day. Much of the brush work is made in single strokes without manipulating the brush to model them. A drawing of this size obviously must omit detail. The flat pattern of shape and tone are what decides its structure—no attempt has been made to express textures. (Original size 7 × 5 in.)

Choosing a suitable subject for the medium you are practising in is most important. The prevailing light conditions are a factor which you cannot ignore, especially when working outside. The play of light on a subject can often be its most appealing aspect and its effects can vary quite dramatically – for instance it may bring out the forms of your subject, or it may flatten them. When you have found a subject which you like enough to attempt a drawing you may find it helpful to ask yourself a few questions before actually putting pen or brush to paper.

The first of these questions should be to consider which viewpoint you should draw from; you should aim for an interesting abstract arrangement of shape, tone and line which also shows the characteristics of the subject best. Other decisions you will learn to make will be concerned with the actual treatment you employ in expressing the nature of whatever you are studying. For example the tracery of winter trees or the texture of a bird's feathers may be best suited to a linear approach, whereas cloud formations may suggest the use of brush and wash. Broken-down buildings, where a myriad of textures may be found, could perhaps be expressed by using a combination of brush, pen and even scraping through solid areas of black with a knife.

Should you wish to capture the particular atmosphere of a place in a drawing then a tonal approach may well be considered. The pattern of light and dark colours expressed in their tonal equivalents can often help to put this across, though on occasions the form of part of your subject may suffer. It is essential to realise that when drawing, or painting, one must be aware that it is not possible to portray every aspect of a subject – some things will have to be subordinate to others. A work which attempts to express everything often loses its unity.

Appearance

Drawing is about seeing and when you can look at things properly and without preconceptions of how they should appear your drawings will improve. We all tend to look at isolated bits of whatever environment we may be a part of. Our view sometimes jumps from one detail to another in the way we may browse through a shop, looking first at one thing, then the next. In drawing it is better to take in the whole vista however large or small it may be and conceive it as a whole. Once able to see in this way relationships between objects and their values of light and dark become much more obvious. When a person invents a picture it is conceived as a whole, thereby expressing the 'idea'. When the novice draughtsman works from direct observation this wholeness of concept often becomes lost in the quest for a pleasing surface appearance of parts of the picture. Though these surface textures of individual elements are important in picture making they must take second place to its construction. Otherwise it would be like painting the bricks of a house individually before erecting the walls.

Working out of doors can present its own problems. Not only the shifting light and weather conditions but also such practical things as how much equipment to take and how large a drawing should be attempted.

It is generally better to sit down when working with washes; for obvious reasons the board or sketch-book must be held as flat as possible. One really needs an easel to work standing up and so perhaps the best thing to do is purchase a small folding stool – the lightest one you can find. Make sure you can sit on it without your knees pointing upwards, this does not help the circulation and it can become most uncomfortable after only a short period of sitting.

The water you will need is best contained in an unbreakable vessel. If you have two tops for it, one can be used when carrying the water, whilst the other can have a small hole bored in it, big enough for a brush to go through. The reason for a small hole is to avoid spilling all the water when you knock the pot over! It can be most frustrating to be without water and not even a stream in sight. This arrangement makes an extra bottle of water unnecessary, saving weight and knapsack space.

Very large sketchbooks are impractical for outdoor work as they tend to be too floppy. A large drawing should be carried out by pinning paper or Bristol board to a lightweight drawing board.

Always take an extra jumper and waterproof hat and coat – the weather can change quickly, and even on a sunny day it can be quite cold in the shade, should you wish to draw there.

Once on site make a few notes in your sketchbook of your subject from different angles and distances until you are satisfied that you know the best view of it and how much of the surrounding environment you think is needed.

For some of you it may be a help to map in some of the larger shaded areas with pencil or diluted ink. I have heard of artists who use maybe three or four bottles of different strength diluted ink and they build up their drawing in this fashion, dispensing with the need for water.

Whatever other bad habits the student pen and ink draughtsman may have, the first to be rid of is timidity. So do not worry about any mistakes, especially at the outset, as these can always be eliminated later if desired. The fact that the marks you will be putting down are so positive make you consider perhaps that little bit more before committing them to the paper; also if they are wrong it is much more apparent and they can be tackled and put right immediately.

Although in some cases it may be possible to complete a drawing on site it is more usual to complete the work in the studio. The work which is done on site will be used as information towards a new completely separate drawing. Working out of doors requires not only concentration, but a logical attitude to why you are there and what you want to come away with. Obviously time is a great factor here and so do not take on too much. Also try to limit your first outdoor studies to working on small areas of the landscape or townscape. Collect enough information to take back to the studio which you can use either towards another drawing or perhaps in a painting.

The type of subject which I would recommend would be a mixture of both natural and man-made forms, such as trees around houses, fences, and boats. The man-made parts of your subject will help to give an idea of scale in the same way that figures would. Apart from setting a scale to the work the introduction of these man-made elements establishes contrast. From a practical point of view the straight edges of buildings both horizontal and vertical will help you to establish the right angles and curves of the geometry of the natural elements. I have also found it useful to begin a drawing by using a vertical or horizontal direction and relating angles to it.

Once you have the basic structure of your drawing complete and have established the large masses of tone in wash, then you should begin to work into the drawing. This is usually best done by working up from the darkest areas you want and carefully relating each section to the next. As the drawing grows and areas begin to look convincing you will find that there are parts which you need not touch any more and others which will need quite a lot of attention. When you are building up darks either with pen or brush wait until the area is dry before applying the next set of strokes or wash. With cross-hatching the small areas of the paper which remain white give the darks a luminosity. When the pen is used wet over wet the lines tend to bleed into each other and blots begin to form and destroy the evenness of the cross-hatching. Solid areas applied with the pen tend to look a bit scruffy and are better put down with a solid wash.

The drawings which you do from direct observation are called studies. The study is the most valuable drawing to the artist because it is the one where he cannot deceive himself and where he will learn how to improve. The study is sometimes referred to as a working drawing and can be used as a method for collecting the right information about a particular thing or aspect of your subject. It must not be thought of as precious finished work.

Now that you have collected enough data about your subjects on the spot it is time to set up in the studio. Either stretch a fairly large sheet of good hand-made paper or select a good size Bristol board (Imperial – or half). Make sure you have plenty of clean water available and that you are not cramped. Your drawings and sketchbook notes should be arranged close at hand for easy reference.

Composition

The rules of composition, that is the rules of design, are many. There are lots of areas to explore and investigate. The most fundamental consideration is that you arrange the elements of your picture into an order which will lead the viewer into the space and around the objects in the picture, and not simply from one side to the other. There are many ways to achieve this, and though I can point to a few and advise on what not to do, you will find it a great help to study and analyse pictures by artists whom you admire. Look for the ways in which they have positioned different elements so the viewer is guided through the picture by suggestions of movement inwards – a path, a fence or a river are often used. Figures often look, or are walking, into the space and rarely out of it.

Other considerations which will need careful forethought before the larger drawing is undertaken will be how much foreground and how much

A

B

C

D

These drawings, made on the spot, took about three hours to complete. Drawing 'A' is a record of the linear aspects, and though crude it serves its purpose. It contains everything which the artist considered important that could be translated into linear terms. The planks of the hull of the large boat, though imprecisely drawn, convey sufficient about their structure to be corrected later in the studio.

'B' concerns itself with the tonal effect of the water. It was drawn in three washes, a fourth being used to pick out some of the darkest areas.

'C' is a fifteen-minute sketch of the whole composition, and deals with the large masses of tone. It contains all of the important structures that will form the basis of the finished drawing.

'D' shows details of the mastheads and skyline.

This shows the beginning of the finished drawing for transfer to canvas. Waterproof ink was used for the pen work and non-waterproof for the washes. It is probably better to use the pen and the brush side by side at first. When a pen drawing is made and then washed over, or vice versa, a disunity often occurs if the artist is inexperienced.

The drawing was begun by establishing the horizontal of the roofs to the left of the composition by relating it to the bottom edge of the paper. From this the vertical direction of the forward mast could be more easily assessed. Once this definite relationship was fixed, finding the correct angle of the deck was fairly easy. It can be seen that the position of the masts was tentatively plotted by the use of dotted lines before making them more positive by using wash. It can also be observed in this drawing that not all the shapes are contained by pen lines. Those which lie back in the composition are treated as simple flat shapes. Rather than treating the water as a moving translucent reflective surface the artist has approached its explanation by thinking of it as an area of abstract shape and tone, and hopefully it has ended up as a representation of water. The use of dry brush technique was helpful, laid over the previous washes. A lot of care has been taken with the silhouette shapes of the chimney stacks on the skyline, and the masts of the boat. The abstract role which they play in the composition, as verticals, helps greatly in balancing an almost entirely horizontal arrangement of shapes. They also help to create new negative shapes by the form of the rigging.

sky are wanted. Taking the first of these; if you are going to have a foreground which is close to the picture plane it must have been carefully studied. It is quite negative to try and make up a foreground of say grasses and flowers without information, so make sure you have sufficient to work from – if not go back to the spot. The sky is often the element most instrumental in setting the mood or atmosphere of a picture. Constable wrote:

> That landscape painter who does not make his skies a very material part of his composition, neglects to avail himself of one of his greatest aids.

However, not all landscape or townscape works have skies. This is an important point to remember. Not all 'landscapes' need skies. The mysteries of wooded landscapes may perhaps be better explored by using only the smallest glimpse of a light sky in order to relieve the darks and help the distance.

The repetition of shape in drawing can both help and bore the viewer. Should you be drawing a subject where there are many vertical directions which you wish to express as lines, then these must be balanced by horizontals and diagonals. These need not necessarily be lines, they may be horizontal solid shapes or tones or a broken abstract movement through the picture. A picture, though, must create its own symmetry. Achieving this balance without disuniting the differing elements is a part of composition which will take a long time to master. With time and study you will gradually improve the design of your drawing.

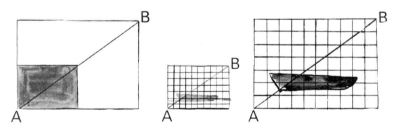

To enlarge a drawing proportionately lay its dimensions at the bottom left-hand corner of a larger sheet. Then draw a diagonal, 'ab'. Any two lines parallel to the edges of your picture when they meet on this diagonal will describe a rectangle of the exact proportions of your drawing, but larger.

To square up mark regular squares on 'ab' of your small drawing. These can then be transferred as in drawing 'A'. It only remains for you to then transfer each part of your drawing to its corresponding square on the large sheet.

Rhythm is very important to drawing. It is part of composition and helps lead the eye around the picture, and also to points which the artist considers significant and not to be missed. This drawing represents part of a composition and was made to separate some of the main rhythms which tree branches formed. Pattern also comes into this drawing—there are quite a few angles repeated. These also help to create movement. The wash was used to help sort out a scale of tone. The square to the right of the right-hand tree is out of scale and jumps out of its place. No attempt was made to make this drawing represent trees—it is merely a search for rhythm and tone.

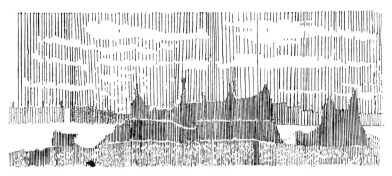

A graphic effect made by ruled lines, some broken, but all of them parallel. Though this kind of drawing is illustrative, the technique dictates that the artist must create a tonal scale to use it to any advantage, and must also be rigorously selective.

two contours the same

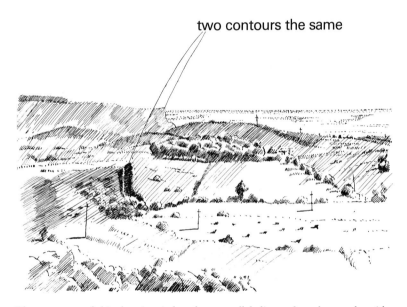

The structure of this drawing is based on parallel diagonal strokes made with a mapping pen. There are no contour lines as such, and though it is a 'line' drawing the effect is tonal.

The broken edges help to create a sunlight effect. The distant sea is made up by stipling—and this again helps to give an effect of sunlight. Notice too the role played by telegraph poles and their shadows. Shapes often repeat themselves in nature; if you find them they can be very useful aids to composition.

Sometimes it may be profitable to select only a small area of your outdoor studies to work up to a finished drawing. By marking different areas using four pieces of paper and trying different-sized frames around them, you can try different compositions.

When choosing your first outdoor subjects remember to choose something which you think you can manage, and make sure that it is possible for it to be translated into the terms which you will be working in. Though ambition is vital to good work, a humble subject can be treated just as ambitiously as a grand one.

The most difficult areas of a drawing are usually those in the foreground. How much foreground you choose to put in is a personal consideration. Here are a few pointers in deciding. Firstly ask yourself if you need a foreground of any size – how significant is it to the point of the drawing? The foreground area is important because it helps the distance or space to work. However the foreground in your picture may, in fact, be some distance from you in actual truth. You do not have to draw from your feet back. It

Sometimes silhouettes can be both dramatic and informative. With one tone and contour quite a lot about the character of this building has been conveyed— including, without actually showing a figure, the suggestion that it is occupied.

may be sufficient to have your foreground beginning 20–30 metres (60–100 ft) in front of you. This can be a great help as the detail is simplified into larger areas of tone and texture. From this kind of distance it is easier to identify the tonal structure as a pattern of light and dark.

This drawing was made with a cartridge drawing pen and concerns itself with the rhythm of the trees, which is why the foreground is very slight. Parts of the trees on the right were redrawn by sticking a clean piece of paper over the offending marks. As you can see it is very difficult to detect.

Rembrandt. *An encampment by the roadside.* Reed pen and bistre wash
(British Museum)

Vincent Van Gogh. *Tile works at Arles*. Reed pen

(Courtauld Institute, London)

John Constable. *On the Stour*. Sepia and brush

(Victoria and Albert Museum)

Claude Lorrain. *A road under a wooded slope.* Pen, brush and brown ink
(British Museum)

Claude Lorrain. *The Tiber above Rome.* Brush and brown wash

(British Museum)

Samuel Palmer. *Shepherds under a full moon*. Brush in Indian ink heightened with white over brown penwork

(Ashmolean Museum, Oxford)

Still life subjects

Still life, for many newcomers to drawing and indeed painting, is a subject which is often either loved or loathed. Perhaps this is because there are so many clichés of still life painting around – bottles, folded clothes and the like. However, there are many interesting ways of treating still life subjects which can be discovered by being bold and experimenting. The only reason for not drawing this or any subject is if you cannot see with your own vision. The way you treat a subject and what you find new in it is what is important. The areas you stress or play down will be decided exclusively by the way you see the subject. In the illustrations on page 40 I have taken the same subject and treated it in a number of different ways. There are many other ways you could treat this very same subject.

Still life subjects can range from anything from flowers to bones and skulls. Animals' skulls can be fairly easily acquired from the butcher. One way to clean them is by burying them in the ground where the insects will do

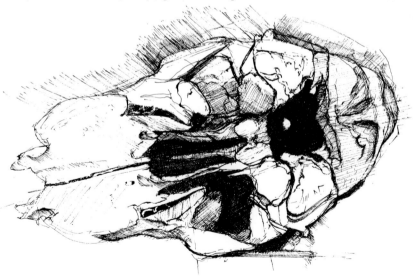

the job. This method, although lengthy – it takes about one year—leaves the bones a gentle ochre colour. A quicker method is to submerge the bone in a diluted acid after boiling the meat parts off. They are fascinating items to study and will certainly test your skill as a draughtsman.

Rather than setting up a still life, which can look contrived if you are not careful in the arrangement, you should look out for natural groupings of things which you think make a pleasing composition. The garden shed and workshop are ideal places to find good compositions of this type, the tools having been left where they were laid down when work stopped. This approach also helps in relating the objects to their particular function and natural environment. A still life of hammers, nails, screws and wood planes set up in front of an ornate mirror on a dressing table amongst perfume bottles, though possible, would probably look a little odd.

Learning about the fundamentals of drawing and getting to understand the different media through still life makes good practice for when you can spend time outside working. The problems of quantity can be eliminated to a certain extent and also the decisions of selection. For first practice in drawing it can be an enormous help both in getting to know the medium

This is a useful subject when making the transition to working outside. Pencil and charcoal are used here.

and learning about proportion. It can give you the confidence to go out and draw. Good subjects to help you make the change from indoor inanimate objects to those which you will be concerned about in the field are branches of trees which have been broken off by the wind, old and knotted pieces of wood, and stones. These are perfect for indoor studies and will help greatly in your understanding of any work you wish to do outside.

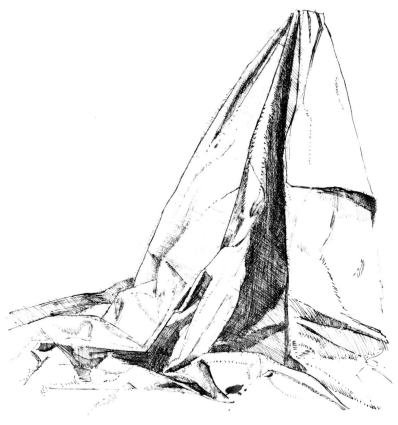

The cross-hatching in this drawing follows the form. When a subject is this complex one of the best ways to approach it is to look for the pattern of light and dark and any geometric shapes which may help to establish it. The study of such a subject is greatly facilitated by forgetting about it being cloth and concentrating on its 'landscape', i.e. its form.

The abstract patterns formed by folds can make exciting additions to drawings and paintings, but in order to learn about them it is important to search them out by being bold.

Figure drawing

Figure drawing is certainly the most demanding subject for the artist. Perhaps one of the most interesting features a study of past artists' work reveals is the singular treatments and 'ideals' they used to express the human form.

The study of the human form has always been a great inspiration to artists and it is the one aspect of painting and drawing which has never gone out of fashion.

In this book it is not my intention to lay down any formulae for the rendering of figures, either clothed or naked. Learning to see and read the gestures of people, and noting the way they express themselves in ways other than speech is the most valuable asset you should endeavour to avail yourself of. Perhaps it is no coincidence that the English have produced many fine writers and few painters, whereas the Italians, noted for their expressive animation, have produced some of the most sublime paintings of human nature. This body language, as it has been called, has always fascinated artists, and they have used it to help express the deepest emotions that we are capable of feeling.

Of course, this is not the only requisite for drawing the figure, but a study of the work of great figure painters will reveal much of this aspect. The face is perhaps the most emotive part of ourselves, yet the positions of our limbs and general posture can add much to the expression. The hands especially can add, for instance, grace or rusticity. Thinking along these lines is important if you are going to pursue a serious study of figure drawing. Again it is important for you not to become bogged down in the reproduction of surface texture to the detriment of other more essential qualities.

As with drawing still life or landscape, the principal element of figure drawing is to establish the basic proportions of the big shapes and tones. This is the area where every novice and indeed 'accomplished' draughtsmen find the greatest difficulties.

Using diluted ink and pen for your first attempts at figure drawing and gradually building the drawing up may help if you are still a little intimidated by the medium.

For many of you, obtaining a model will be a problem. It is very difficult to find a model willing to pose for hours, even more so if you need to draw nudes. Joining a life drawing class at your local evening education centre is the best answer to this one; otherwise perhaps an understanding friend may help out occasionally. Failing this one always has oneself, and investment in one or two large mirrors can help a great deal; it is at least better than no model at all. Costume models are easier to find, and a little easier to draw to begin with.

A clothed model can be a very exciting subject and you can learn a lot. When a person is clothed the subtleties of the naked form are concealed, and the big shapes and changes are more easily identified. Clothes also give clues to the underlying structure. A necklace, a cuff, or a belt around the model's waist hint at the underlying form because they are identified in visual terms as being part ellipses and circles. Their form suggests a cross-section of the form they are covering. Many nudes, in fact, have a bracelet or other such device which helps to put this across. The bottoms of trousers and the ellipses they form around the ankle should also be observed carefully – as should shoes, especially where they fit around the ankle.

The most common way of expressing form in pen drawing is to use cross-hatching. In figure drawing especially it is not simply a question of hatching in the right tones and shapes. The directions of the strokes must 'follow the form'. What this term refers to is the way that a plane falls away or comes forward.

Try to confine your first studies of figures to explaining in the most graphic terms what the figure is doing. A person sitting down, for example, is most easily depicted by taking a side view. A walking figure would also be best expressed by a profile. The basic idea of a figure with outstretched arms would be most graphically shown by being drawn from the front or back. These are obvious examples, and worth noting because when an inexperienced draughtsman is making a drawing of, for example, a sitting figure from the front the tendency is to make the thighs too long, and to increase the angle at the knee.

The reason for this is that we automatically try to convey actualities. One of the biggest stumbling blocks to overcome is that of trying to put down how something really is, instead of how it appears to the artist. An outstretched arm, for example, viewed directly on, is only known to be longer than the head because of what is called foreshortening. This is perspective of the figure, and its effects can be very beautiful as well as dramatic. Occasionally when looking at foreshortened figures the distortion is so subtle that it is almost impossible for it to work in a drawing. Always look carefully at any foreshortened areas of the figure you may be drawing from, and ask yourself if they will work in a drawing. Relating a foreshortened figure to the surroundings is vital, especially if the figure is lying down.

Because drawing is a means of communication it is essential that you keep in mind the basic idea you wish to communicate to the viewer. Because figure drawing is new to you it will help you to draw those poses and actions

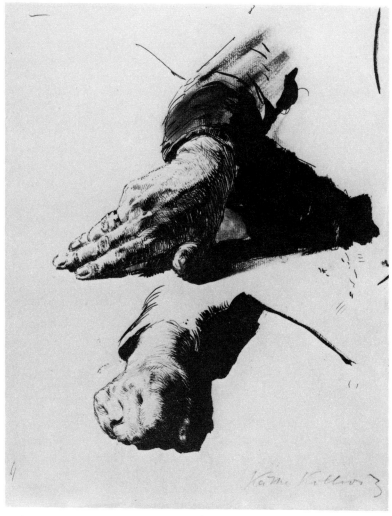

Kathë Kollwitz. *Study of hands*

(British Museum)

which you can more easily visualise as a two-dimensional image. Something else you may find helpful at first is choosing actions and activities which you are yourself familiar with. For example, one flute player drawing another would be most conscious of the positions of both arms and fingers and would be likely to pay more attention to this aspect of the drawing than, say, a footballer would. The knowledge we already have about familiar activities is important. Drawing from these will not only be good practice but will also give confidence, which you will need in order to tackle more complex poses and groups of figures.

Pen and ink is used to a great extent in commercial art. Its graphic qualities make it ideal for reproduction. Many illustrations both technical and picturesque are first rendered in pen and ink or pen and wash. There are a number of periodicals and comics with illustrations of this kind and they are always worth looking at. Old copies of magazines like *The Illustrated London News* have excellent drawings and black and white prints as illustrations.

Techniques

The techniques employed in the drawing of figures in ink are varied. In this section I shall illustrate some of the most widely used. However, this is only a starting point; it will be more profitable for you to work in your own way once you have understood the elementary procedures involved in the medium.

Cross-hatching Possibly the oldest technique of working in pen is cross-hatching. If you have followed the instructions on how to achieve an even cross-hatching then you should have no difficulty in adapting this method to figure work. Rather than simply building up the tone in a mechanical way as when drawing regular-shaped subjects such as box shapes, in figure drawing try to make the lines you do use help to explain the form by following the way a plane falls. Make lots of drawings of your own features and keep in mind that it is the form of your head and not a 'likeness' which is the main objective.

Line Line drawing heads and figures in ink is a particularly precise technique and for your first attempts it may be less frustrating if you make an outline drawing in pencil first. Pay particular attention to those sensitive areas of the head such as the mouth and nostrils. These two areas are immensely difficult points for the beginner and so you should have a clear idea of how you are going to treat the drawing at these particular points. The mouth especially is very subtle and much of it is described by a change of colour. Make separate studies when in doubt, either on another scrap sheet, or else on the side of the paper. The most important line of the mouth is where the bottom lip meets that of the upper; this line is basically curved even when looked at straight on.

Any lines you put down on your paper should signify that something is happening at that point; either the form is changing direction or it has turned completely away, in which case the line marks the visual edge of the plane. Where a change of plane is subtle a dotted line may suffice to explain this. Occasionally, if a strong light is falling on a plane, the edge becomes 'lost' and undefinable against its background. In a line drawing this can be advantageous as you can leave that space blank; the viewer will understand, in the same way that his or her sensibilities will always choose the right line out of any number of possibilities – even though it may be subconscious.

The modelled line in figure drawing can be used to good advantage. For instance the creases of the eyelids may suggest a thicker line where the lid turns away 'into' the socket. The line of the mouth, especially if the lips are not completely closed tight, would warrant this type of line. When the form of a limb appears more prominent a strengthening of line may be required.

Whether you use a brush or a pen for this type of drawing is really a personal matter, as it is equally suited to both. However, as it takes much longer than one thinks to get to know how to use the tools of drawing, do not try to work in a slick fashion. What I mean by this is do not worry if you cannot make the line express the form by dashing down a contour in one gesture, trying to achieve the degrees of change by pressure of the pen or brush. Though in time it will be possible for you to achieve this kind of immediacy of execution, attempting it at this stage for figure work will lead to frustration. The brush is most suitable for swift drawing of modelled lines as it can be manipulated by adding pressure. A steel pen is not particularly good as it can splatter the ink all over if too much pressure is applied. When the steel pen is used for a modelled line, the thicker parts should be built up by drawing two lines close to each other. A reed pen or quill is more suitable than the steel nib as these are much softer and more pliable – being midway between brush and steel nib.

Stipple   The stippling technique of ink drawing is used fairly frequently in advertising illustrations as it is most suitable for reproduction. The figure or head is drawn by using a series of dots – no lines are used and it is a technique which has certain affinities with the structure of newspaper photographs which are themselves made up from a series of dots. The tones are achieved by placing the dots in varying degrees of saturation. A very dark area would be almost entirely covered in them whereas lighter tones of course would

This head was drawn on Ingres paper. Where possible the shapes have been defined as flat areas of tone. A very fine brush was used for the hatching. Pencil was used to lay out the larger shapes. Using a brush to cross-hatch enables the artist to use greys, rather than the jet black ink which would have to be used with a pen.

have few, if any. It gives a drawing a certain grainy texture and can be very effective when it works. However, it is a technique which needs careful preparation and you should have a fairly good plan made out as to how many tones you want to use and also the size.

Remember that, although you may see a drawing 5 cm (2 in) square in your magazine, the artist would probably have made the original considerably larger, and so the detail perhaps is not quite as mind-boggling as one may at first think! I find this technique very boring to actually execute. The important thing to remember is no matter whether the tone is light or dark, the dots must be regularly spaced and all the same size to achieve even tones. If you find this technique to your own liking, it may be worth while investing in a cartridge drawing pen as these are ideal for this type of mechanical technique.

Wash in figure drawing   Using wash as a medium for figure drawing is ideal. The subtleties of tonal change often needed in the portraying of gentle rounded surfaces make it particularly suitable. Pen and wash work together excellently in the expression of human form.

Possibly one of the simplest ways of using wash for this subject is in a fairly light key to begin with. Using only the brush, lay down a wash simplifying the form into its basic geometric shapes. Begin by establishing the torso area and work out from there. Always keep in mind the negative shapes and use them to assist with the relationship of limbs to body, and also use anything behind the figure that will help you to gauge distances and proportions.

Wash is often used in conjunction with other media, charcoal, crayon and pencil. Try them out and see whether you like them.

Some artists prefer to draw the linear aspects of their subjects prior to laying on washes, and others find it easier to put down the general tones and proportions before picking out specific points with the pen. However, I would recommend using wash first if you are not very experienced.

At first you will make some pretty awful drawings! But do not be deterred, as this is a part of learning, and goes hand in hand with enquiry. An attitude of determination and dedication is needed, more in figure drawing than in anything else.

A change in a regular pattern makes us look for the reason why. Why is that figure looking down, and what at? Why is he smiling?

Five marks—when placed in a certain relationship to each other form a pictogram of a face.

The 'idea' of a face is expressed in its most basic form. An elementary consideration perhaps, but one which is more important than any other in drawing heads. The distortion from this schema decides the visual character of a subject.

Opposite

A. Depending on what is added, and how the 'extras' are distorted, a different feeling is conveyed.

B. Notice here that the nose is widened, the eyes are open more fully.

C. The long face has a long and narrow nose.

D. Slightly more sophisticated, these drawings perhaps show something more particular—the astronomer so used to looking through his telescope continues to affect the distortion of his features even away from his work.

Everything about the middle figure is sharp and pointed and has an effect on the viewer. Who would you invite to tea with only appearance to judge by? I would invite the open-eyed, round-faced girl, her dimples perhaps hint at a face which often smiles.

E. This character tries to disguise himself but is betrayed by tell-tale points; his nose, moustache, even the form of the collar.

A

B

C

D

An ASTRONOMER? WHO WOULD YOU INVITE TO TEA?

E

All of these drawings are quite basic and deal entirely with reaction to shape and type. The caricaturist relies on us being indoctrinated to some extent and perhaps figure D and figure E are quite pleasant and generous characters—but visually they do not inspire us to trust them.

Clues are important: is the stooping figure begging from the smart gentleman? Another clue, the rain, shows that he isn't, he is feeling the raindrops.

The side view of a man digging is much more informative than the front view.

Many caricaturists distort and stretch our comprehension to its limits. One would rarely come across a figure which looked like 'A' or 'B' yet they remain recognizable human beings. 'C' and 'D' are very far-fetched representations of human anatomy—but again they do their job.

'E' is a brush drawing; the hair is quite extraordinary and 'unreal' yet these marks give a life to the drawing and a sense of the wind—which is accentuated by the collar.

'F' shows a very bad drawing if we consider contour—the guns are ridiculous—but the 'idea' is put across: the big man towers over the small man. His stance is 'manly' and strong, everything about him overpowers the smaller man knocking at the knees, his head almost buried into his shoulders. He also stands under the shadow of Terrible Tex.

A

B

C

'A' is a study made looking into a bright light. There is a lot wrong with this drawing, and some of the light areas have been re-touched with white gouache. When a subject leans his face against something it inevitably will be distorted to some extent. It is however a drawing which concerns itself with the effect of light, and as such exactness of contour is secondary. There is no reason why minor mistakes should not be corrected without the model. Do not get bogged down, and keep to the point; in this drawing it was essential to find the lights and darks.

'B' shows a drawing made with a mapping pen. It is a carefully measured drawing. Perhaps the most remarkable thing about such drawings is that the shapes end up looking like something. In this drawing notice the eyes, especially the right one, and also that there is no eyebrow to the left eye—only its direction is marked. Does it matter that the hair is not illustrated at this point?

'C' shows the effect stippling produces when applied to figure drawing. It may be advantageous to lightly draw in the large shapes with a pencil before using the ink.

This drawing would be ideal for translation into the large shapes of lino cutting. Much can be learnt by such a bold and selective approach to drawing.

Executed with pencil and brush these drawings show to some extent how a keen eye for geometry can help explain enough about the shape and tone of form to express surface anatomical structure. The dark area to the right of the top figure helps to bring out the light of the shoulder. If you do this in your own work be careful that you do not end it abruptly as this can often distract and look ugly. Try to wash the edge out so that it is soft and unnoticeable.

Scraperboard is a technique whereby the image is scraped away, leaving a white area. Special board is needed which can be purchased from most art materials stockists. This board is covered with Indian ink and when dry and brittle the image is revealed by scraping through it. There are special scraper tools available. This image however was made using an ordinary pen. Its effects can be not unlike a wood engraving and it is a useful medium in which to work out designs for engraving, especially as any mistakes can easily be rectified by covering up offending marks with ink and re-scraping.

This study was made as a working drawing. The figures have been distorted in an attempt to make them more monumental.

The edges of the pond on either side of the arch differ in character; the left-hand edge is a winter scene and is jagged and 'cold' whereas the right-hand pond edge is much more rounded and 'warm'. The rods of the fishermen help direct the viewer towards the central figure and on to each side. Notice how the two extreme tree trunks lean into the composition.

Pencil, ink, charcoal and watercolour were used.

Michelangelo. *Nude youth with left arm extended*. Pen and brown ink
(British Museum)

Michelangelo. *Head of a satyr*. Pen and two shades of brown ink

(British Museum)

Rembrandt. *Self portrait*. Pen and bistre, brush and Indian ink. Bistre is a sooty and impermanent medium Rembrandt often used with pen

(British Museum)

Rembrandt. *Girl sleeping*. Brush and bistre wash
(British Museum)

Jules Chadel. *Figure resting*. Brush drawing   (British Museum)

Rembrandt. *Female nude surrounded by drapery*. Pen and wash in bistre and ink
(British Museum)

Rembrandt. *Study of a male nude standing*. Pen and bistre and wash, heightened with
white gouache   (British Museum)